OUR
MYSTERIOUS
WORLD

by DJ Arneson and Tony Tallarico

Watermill Press

Our world abounds with mysteries. Some are huge puzzles. Some are just confusing. But taken together, they remind us that the universe is a much more interesting place in which to live than we sometimes think.

Are there such things as flying saucers? Do strange giants walk the earth? Is it possible to see into the future? Can people come back from the dead? Are dreams real? Do aliens from outer space visit our planet?

These and many other questions interest investigators. They also interest the rest of us. And so they should, for even though it is possible that not all of the peculiar reports made by startled people through history are real, it is certainly possible that some of them are.

Which reports are true and which are not? Perhaps we shall never know. But that doesn't stop us from wondering.

Here, for your wondering pleasure, are just a few of the thousands of strange, weird things of our mysterious world.

Space Monster???

The five young friends stared skyward. High above them a wobbling, spark-shooting disc flew slowly through the evening sky. It glided to a landing on a nearby mountain top, hidden by trees.

The youngsters thought an emergency had occurred. They raced home. When they were joined by one of the mothers and a teen-aged boy, the group decided to investigate the strange sighting.

When they approached the site of the landing, which was marked by a pulsing red glow in the sky, they were struck by an irritating odor which drifted around them in a thin fog. Then they spied the object. It was a large, saucer-shaped device about 25 feet in diameter. They watched it in amazement.

Suddenly a movement in the bushes startled them. The teen-ager turned his flashlight in the direction of the noise. The light stopped. Caught in its beam was a ten-foot tall creature with a round, red face in a helmet. It stared at the shuddering group through green-orange eyes that reflected light like a cat's.

The group raced for safety. When they returned with the sheriff, the smell was still there. But the creature and its amazing machine were gone. But gone. . .where?

The Strangest Voyage

The *Mermaid's* sails began to flutter. Then they filled with wind. A sudden, terrible storm had come from nowhere. The ship fought valiantly, but it was no use. It split in half and sank, spilling its 22 crewmen and passengers into the roaring waves.

Amazingly, a large outcrop of rock was within reach. All 22 survivors reached its safety. They hung onto the barren rock for three days. Then a ship, the *Swiftsure,* found them and rescued all 22.

The *Swiftsure* sailed peacefully for 5 days. Without warning it was swept into an uncharted current and smashed against rocks. Everyone was pitched into the sea. But once again, not a life was lost. They staggered onto a barren beach.

A few hours later the *Governor Ready's* sails came into view. The two boatloads of survivors were saved. But luck was not with them. Three hours later the *Governor Ready* caught fire. Survivors and rescuers abandoned ship.

When the *Comet* appeared, three boatloads of survivors were rescued. And still not a soul was lost.

The men on board the *Comet* were afraid. They were certain that the shipwrecked group was a jinx.

So, when a powerful blast of wind tore off the *Comet's* mast and stripped her of her rudder, her

crew abandoned her. They left the three ships' worth of survivors on board the drifting hulk to fend for themselves.

Eighteen hours later the *Jupiter* found the helpless group. Four shipwrecks had been endured and not a single life was lost.

An old woman on the *Jupiter* looked up at the bedraggled survivors. She was Sarah Richey, who had traveled all the way from England to Australia to search for her son, Peter, who had disappeared 15 years earlier.

Peter, a crewman on the *Mermaid*, smiled back at his mother. They were reunited in the strangest of all sea voyages.

Is it possible that all lives were spared to ensure Peter's safe return to the arms of his aging mother?

Monster or Myth?

People have suspected something strange in the waters of Loch Ness in Scotland for more than a thousand years. Fear kept suspicions quiet for centuries. But in 1933 fear came into the open. "An enormous animal" was spotted in the waters of the cold, extremely deep lake. Since that time, hundreds of sightings have been made. And many photographs of an unexplainable thing in the water have been made.

The "thing" is called Nessie, the Loch Ness Monster. What is it? Is it seaweed gathered in a heap as some say? Is it a dolphin or a seal? Or is it a prehistoric creature thought to be extinct?

Nessie is huge, whatever she is. She has a tiny head on the end of a long, slender neck. She propels herself through the water by triangular shaped flippers.

No carcass of a dead "Nessie" has ever been found. But neither has the body of anyone unfortunate enough to drown in the 600 foot deep lake ever been found.

Scientific expeditions have explored the lake from end to end. Photographs of dark, ominous shapes have been made. And sonar soundings of the long, narrow lake have revealed unexplained shapes beneath the surface.

What are they? Where did they come from? Is Nessie a *plesiosaur,* presumed extinct for 70 million years?

Skeptics abound, but scientific evidence suggests very strongly that Nessie is real. And alive. If so, she is still there. Waiting and watching.

Lost Memory?

Barney and Betty Hill were driving home very late one night when they saw a peculiar light in the sky. They stopped their car to watch it. A large disc rimmed with a double row of windows hummed above the frightened couple. They drove off, determined to get away from the huge craft.

Suddenly the car was filled with an odd beeping sound. The car began to vibrate. The Hills became drowsy.

Two hours later they were wide awake. They were 35 miles from where they had been. And neither one of them could remember what had happened during the lost two hours.

The incident disturbed Mr. and Mrs. Hill. Betty Hill had dreams that she had been aboard a flying saucer. Barney grew nervous, as if something was troubling him.

Under hypnosis the worried couple revealed memories of their lost two hours. Small creatures with smooth domed heads had taken them aboard the huge disc. They had been examined by the creatures with instruments never seen nor heard of on earth. When the examinations were over, the confused couple were told to forget everything. The spacecraft took off.

Will it return? Was it ever really here? Researchers disagree. But the Hills don't!

Gone. . .Forever?

David Lang paused in an empty field near his farm house. He waved to his wife and children who were waiting for him. On a nearby road a friend, Judge Peck, drove up in his horse and buggy, with his brother-in-law at his side. Five people watched David Lang wave. They watched him walk six steps across the field. And then they watched him disappear.

David Lang simply stepped off the face of the earth. One second he was there, and the next he was gone.

A massive search was organized. Every inch of
ground was covered. Not a trace of the missing
farmer was found. He had vanished into thin air
in full view of five people.

Seven months later Lang's two children visited
the spot where their father had disappeared. A
circle of short, yellowed grass, unlike the rest in
the field, marked the place. Sarah Lang called her
father's name.

A thin, eery voice replied. "Help. Help," it
called. "Help. . .help. . ." Then the voice faded
away and David Lang was gone. . .forever?

Runaway Reactor?

It was an explosion unlike any other ever seen on earth. A brilliant streak of light flashed through the sky. Suddenly, it exploded. The sun turned dark. A powerful blast swept the countryside. Millions of sturdy trees toppled. The blast wave traveled around the whole world. *Twice!* People over 37 miles away were knocked to the ground. The sound of the explosion was heard over 1000 kilometers away. For many nights the sky was bright. It was possible to read a newspaper at midnight.

The explosion was almost identical to a thermonuclear blast, a hydrogen bomb. But the year was 1908! No nation on earth would construct a hydrogen bomb until almost 50 years later.

What was this strange, unearthly explosion that destroyed thousands of square miles of forest and threw millions of tons of dust into the air?

Nobody knows. The blast occurred in the remote regions of Siberia. Very few people witnessed the fiery flash. Scientific investigations weren't begun for many years.

Was it a comet? A huge bit of anti-matter? Was it a "black hole" from the farthest reaches of the universe? Or was it something quite different? Is it possible that the mysterious Tunguska explosion was caused by intelligent beings?

One theory boggles the mind. It suggests that the blast was the accidental explosion of a spacecraft from outer space, whose nuclear reactor was runaway and out of control. The craft desperately searched for a place to land. Realizing that it was too late to save themselves, the pilots aboard the doomed craft veered its course. They headed for the most unpopulated reaches of Earth. And there they met their awesome fate.

Tunguska. Was it natural. . .or was it something else?

The Hairy Giant of the Northwest

A trail of gigantic footprints leads into the remote forests of Washington State for more than a half a mile. There are over a thousand of them. One foot seems to be crippled.

Two men on horseback photograph a mammoth creature that looks like a hairy ape. It vanishes into the woods.

In ten years, over 300 people report seeing an unbelievable creature in the sparsely inhabited regions of the Pacific Northwest.

The gathered information suggests that a 7-to-9-foot tall, 600 to 900 pound, apelike creature that walks like a man lives in the woods. He has huge, long arms and powerful shoulders. He is covered with thick fur and has feet 16 inches long. It is with good reason that he is called Bigfoot.

Is Bigfoot related to the yeti of the Himalayas? Is he a survivor of another age, the legendary Gigantopithecus, an extinct ape-man?

The Indians of the area don't think so. They have honored Bigfoot, whom they call Sasquatch, which means "hairy man," for centuries. He is carved into their totem poles and spoken of in their folklore.

Scientific expeditions have searched for Bigfoot. A man has even claimed to have been kidnapped by a tribe of the huge creatures.

Bigfoot is not ferocious, people say. He lives quietly in the deep forests. Perhaps he was driven there by the expanding world of 20th Century man. If so, where will he go when men penetrate his private territory? Will he be so peaceful then?

Mystery Ship

Twenty-five people boarded the motorship, *Joyita,* on October 3, 1955. Passengers and crew, they expected to sail from Western Samoa to the Tokelau Islands about 270 miles away. They never arrived.

The *Joyita* was found abandoned 37 days after it had sailed. The ship's provisions, the captain's log and navigation instruments, and a large sum of money were missing. Everything else was intact.

What happened? Was the ship boarded by pirates? Had everyone been swept overboard by a tidal wave? One theory proposed that the ill-fated ship had been visited by creatures from outer space who had kidnapped the passengers and crew. Perhaps a deadly storm forced the doomed to abandon ship.

Whatever happened may never be known. But somewhere, far out to sea, the lingering memories of a boatload of people and the truth of the *Joyita's* fatal voyage is engraved upon the waves.

The Canvey Island Creature

The creature was already dead. It had washed ashore on Canvey Island, England. It was two-and-a-half feet tall. It had thick, brown-red skin and a pulpy kind of head with two eyes protruding from it. Though it came from the sea, it had two legs, and at the ends of the legs were feet. It was evident that the creature, whatever it was, could walk upright.

Since nobody knew what the thing was, it was destroyed—but only after photos and studies were made.

Then, about 9 months later, another of the creatures washed ashore. This one was pink, was over four feet long, and weighed 25 pounds. It too had perfect feet on the ends of short, but sturdy legs. Nostril holes, a large, gaping mouth filled with sharp teeth, and a pair of huge eyes made up the thing's "face."

What were they? Where did they come from? Were they really sea creatures? Or had they come from someplace. . .else? Nobody knows.

City Beneath the Sea?

Legends say Atlantis was a continent which vanished into the ocean. It has never been discovered. But a strange find under the waters of the Bahama Islands raises interesting questions.

In 1969, two young investigators located a row of giant, rectangular stones while diving. The stones were unlike any found in nature. In fact,

they resembled building blocks, the kind used to construct city walls. Indeed, the blocks were laid out in such a way that they looked like a wall.

Other divers found even more interesting "evidence" of a sunken city beneath the sea. Pillars, some still standing, were found in the same general area as the stone "wall."

Are these discoveries enough to prove the existence of a place such as Atlantis? They must prove something. But *what*?

A Winning Nightmare

An Englishman who enjoyed betting at the racetrack had a peculiar dream one night. He dreamed that he was in court for a terrible crime. But when the judge in the dream gave the man a very light sentence, the man was extremely grateful. He whispered the name "Solario" to the judge.

The next day the man remembered the dream when he went to the racetrack to bet on the horses. One of the horses was named Solario. The happy man eagerly bet on his "dream" horse.

The horse won and the man, much wealthier, had an odd dream to thank for the good luck.

Can it work for everyone? Why not?

Strange Call for Help

Merna believed her dream. She had had it too many times to doubt it. Each time the dream was the same. In it she saw her boyfriend, Stanislaus, calling for help from inside a dark, dingy ruin. Merna was sure the ruin was a castle.

Merna was a young Polish girl in love with a young Polish soldier who had vanished during the First World War. Merna refused to believe that Stanislaus was dead. Her dream convinced her that he was still alive.

People laughed at Merna when she said she would find Stanislaus. There were hundreds of ruined castles. How could she ever hope to find the right one, even if the dream were true? And how could someone trapped inside survive for nearly two years? It had been that long since Merna first had the dream.

She searched the countryside. She passed ruin after ruin. Then one day she recognized the castle of her dreams. She ran to it. Scoffing townspeople laughed at her frantic efforts to uncover a caved-in section of the castle's tunnel.

Then a distant voice called for help. The stones were pulled away. And inside, trapped for two years with only cheese and wine to eat, was Stanislaus, saved by a young girl who loved him, and a dream.

The Original "Little" Old Man

Charles Charlesworth was born in England in 1829. He was an ordinary baby and grew to become an ordinary little boy. But when Charles was four years old, something quite extraordinary began to happen.

Charles began to grow whiskers. Soon he had a beard. His skin began to wrinkle. He began to stoop over when he walked. In fact, everything about him suggested that he was more like a 70-year-old man than a child. His hair was as white as snow and his veins stood out sharply on his withered arms and legs.

And then, at age seven, "young" Charles Charlesworth suddenly died. The verdict was quite expected. The boy who had barely lived more than half a decade had died. . .of old age!

"Telescopic" Vision

In the mid-1700's a beacon keeper in France claimed to possess the unusual ability to spot ships at sea. The claim may not have been so unusual if the man, Mr. Bottineau, had used a telescope. But even if he had, his strange ability was more than "met the eye."

What made Mr. Bottineau's method remarkable was the fact that he claimed to see ships coming which were still a many days' sail away. "Three ships approaching," he would say, "one from the west, one from the south and one from the north."

Days would pass. Suddenly, sails would appear on the horizon. The ships the unusual beacon keeper had predicted arrived, on schedule.

Nobody has ever learned how he performed his incredible feat of seeing farther than the eye or a telescope ever could. But he proved it, over 500 times!

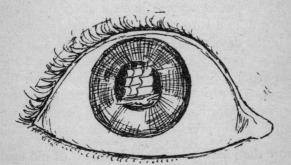

A Ghostly Guard

Beware of stormy nights on White Island, off the coast of New Hampshire. And if it's treasure you seek, beware *doubly*. There's a ghost on guard whose duty it is to chase treasure seekers away.

In the days of Blackbeard the Pirate, Captain Sandy Gordon, a Blackbeard crony, buried the loot from a Spanish galleon somewhere on the island. To protect it, Captain Gordon left his girlfriend Martha behind. Gordon perished in a battle and never returned. But Martha still waits. . .for those who dare! The treasure has never been found.

The Living Earth

Is it possible that the earth is a giant organism, not unlike a planet-sized animal? The Gaia Hypothesis (named after the Greek goddess of the earth) suggests that it is. How can that be?

For life to be maintained on earth, certain conditions must be regulated within very narrow limits. These conditions, such as the amount of water on the earth, the chemical composition of the air, and the alkalinity of the soil, cannot vary too much before life would cease.

The Gaia Hypothesis (a hypothesis is an unproved theory) says that all living organisms on earth cooperate to keep the planet itself alive. Such cooperation would make Mother Earth herself a huge, *living* organism.

Then what about the Universe? Can it too be a living creature?

The Phantom Hitchhikers

The story is repeated over and over, many years apart. But it is always the same.

The road is empty. A lone car travels through the dusk. Suddenly, a hitchhiker appears in the dim glow of the car's headlights. The car stops and picks up the hitchhiker.

The hitchhiker tells the driver an address. As the driver willingly drives to the address, he turns to discover that the hitchhiker has vanished.

Confused, the driver goes to the address. There he learns that the hitchhiker was the ghost of a young person who was killed near the spot where the puzzled motorist first stopped.

Sometimes the story has a young woman as the hitchhiker; sometimes it is a young man. The people who have seen them swear they are real. What would you do, late at night, if a hitchhiker appeared?

Premonition

A strange light glowed at the top of the stairs. Mrs. Wenner-Gren paused. She was puzzled, for all the lights in the big house had been turned off.

Suddenly a figure emerged from the light. It was a man. In his arms was the body of a mortally wounded child. A great red gash cut across the child's forehead.

The event disturbed Mrs. Wenner-Gren. Her husband agreed that she should take a restful cruise aboard their yacht.

Unknown to the Wenner-Grens, the *Athenia,* a large ship, had been torpedoed nearby. It was one of the first such events of the Second World War. The Wenner-Grens went to the aid of survivors.

The first person they rescued was a man. In his arms was a dying child with a terrible gash across its forehead. It was the same pair Mrs. Wenner-Grens had seen in the light at the top of her stairs.

Mystery Shrouded Smuggler's Cove

In 1795 three youths exploring Oak Island off the coast of Nova Scotia found a strange, filled-in shaft. The shaft was clearly manmade. But by whom?

Over the years, many diggers have explored the peculiar shaft in what is sometimes called Pirate's Cove. The shaft is a curious thing. At every ten feet, it is plugged by wood platforms. Some of the platforms have been caulked with coconut fiber. Coconuts do not grow within a thousand miles of Oak Island.

At a depth of 90 feet, a stone slab scribbled with strange markings was discovered. The odd writing has never been deciphered.

An elaborate water tunnel system connects to the mysterious shaft. Water from the tunnels has flooded the shaft. Was this intended to keep treasure seekers from finding whatever lay hidden at the bottom? So far, no one knows.

A Cry for Help

A young boy travelling on a long ocean voyage slipped and fell into the sea. His life was in great danger. He screamed for his mother.

The boy's mother heard his cries. But there was nothing she could do. She was in England, thousands of miles from the drowning boy.

Luckily, the boy was saved. When he returned home, his mother told him what had happened. To her, she said, his shouts had sounded as if he were just down the street.

The End of the Line

In the days of the old West, just about everyone searched for gold. One gold fever victim, a young boy, found something quite different.

The boy became lost in the hills. His burro had wandered off. Town, a long walk away, was the boy's goal.

Trudging along a lonely stagecoach road, the boy listened to the howls of wolves at his back. Then another sound greeted him. A mammoth black stagecoach drawn by magnificent black

horses rounded a bend. The coach stopped. The
driver signalled the boy aboard.

The coach rumbled like the wind toward town.
It stopped to let the boy off. When the boy
turned around, the stagecoach was gone.

The next morning townspeople stood in awe at
a strange sight. Stagecoach tracks pressed in the
dusty road indicated where the stage had come
from. But they ended just where the boy said.
They didn't turn around; they simply vanished.

Where did the phantom stage come from?
Where did it go?

Lincoln's Mirror

After Abraham Lincoln was elected president in 1860, he looked into a mirror on his bureau and was surprised to see two reflections of himself. One was his regular, healthy face. The other was sickly and had a deathly pallor.

Mary, his wife, interpreted the strange vision to mean that her husband would be healthy through his first term of office, but would die during his second term.

Abraham Lincoln was assassinated during his second term of office. Did he know all along that he would die?

The Worst Dream of All

In 1979 a man had a terrifying series of dreams. In his dreams he saw a large airplane roll over slowly and crash to earth. The dream was almost always the same. It was vividly real. In fact, it was so real that the man was unable to sleep. He became extremely nervous. He couldn't work at his job.

The poor man didn't know what to do. Out of desperation he called an official of the Federal Aeronautics Administration, the agency of the government that regulates airlines. He spoke with an official who was perplexed by the series of dreams. But there was nothing either man could do. Though they suspected that they knew which airline the airplane in the dream belonged to, they didn't know when or where it would be flying.

On Memorial Day weekend the worst airline crash in the United States occured at O'Hare International Airport in Chicago. Almost 250 people were killed when a jumbo jet lost an engine, rolled over in the air and plunged to the ground. It was the worst crash and the worst dream imaginable.

Elevator to Oblivion

Lord Dufferin stood quietly at the window of his guest house admiring the moon, and the stars. Restless, he could not sleep, so he waited by the window for his nerves to calm.

A figure appeared in the garden. On his back he carried a coal black coffin. Lord Dufferin was confused and frightened. And, when an investigation revealed nothing, the poor Lord was perplexed.

The incident was forgotten for many years. Then, one day while visiting Paris, Lord Dufferin was about to step into an elevator. He stopped, astounded. The elevator operator was the same man he had seen in the garden. Lord Dufferin quickly jumped out of the elevator.

Seconds later the elevator crashed. Many were killed, including the strange operator. Who was the man Lord Dufferin had seen twice? Nobody knew. The day of the crash was his first day on the job.

Had he been sent as a warning? And if so, from where?

Lost Memory

It was only recently that medical science discovered something which the human body has known for millions of years. It is called the Mammalian Diving Reflex. Understanding it has saved many people from drowning, for it has brought unfortunate victims back from "death."

The MDR, as it is called, is simple. When someone falls face first into extremely cold water, a reflex of the body takes over. The heart slows its beat. Blood no longer flows to all the extremities. Instead, only the heart itself, the brain and the lungs are supplied with life sustaining oxygen. The rest of the body is allowed to go into "suspended animation."

If the victim is pulled from the water in time, sometimes as long as a few hours, and is given resuscitation treatment, the person once doomed can be restored to life.

Is the MDR a forgotten memory? Perhaps. But most important of all, it has saved lives and will continue to do so now that it is understood.

A Voice from the Grave

Little Max Hoffman was only 5 years old when he died of cholera. He was buried in the local cemetery.

In the middle of the night, Max's mother jumped out of bed screaming. She told her husband that she had had a vision of their son. She claimed that the boy was still alive. In her vision she saw the child scratching inside the coffin, trying to get out.

The same dream startled the poor woman awake the next night. This time the husband acted. With some neighbors, he dug up the boy's grave.

Max was lying on his side even though he had been lying on his back when he was buried. Mr. Hoffman took the lifeless body. A doctor was called to examine it.

The doctor detected a weak pulse. It was unbelievable, but the boy was alive. Max's chest

was massaged. Soon he recovered. And in a week he was perfectly normal.

Max lived to be over 80 years old, thanks to a voice from the grave. . .his own.

You Saw It Here First

A well-known Swedish scientist and mystic, Emmanuel Swedenborg, was visiting the city of Goteborg, Sweden. While there, a terrifying vision suddenly came to him. A deadly fire, racing out of control, raged through his home city of Stockholm. Block after block of the city burned as Swedenborg watched the realistic vision.

The strange image of the fire continued for three hours. Then, with a sigh of relief, the scientist relaxed. In his vision, the fire had stopped only a few doors away from his own house.

Later, a messenger from the ill-fated city arrived. All of the details of the mystic's vision were true. He had witnessed a real event while it was happening on the opposite side of the country.

The Village That Vanished

Fur trapper Joe Labelle sensed that something was wrong when he stopped a few feet from the Eskimo village on Lake Anjikuni. "Where are my friends?" he wondered. The village, completely intact, was abandoned.

Cooking pots filled with food hung over dead fires. Rifles, the Eskimos' prize possessions, leaned against hut doorways. Sled dogs, who had died of starvation, were tied up a short distance away.

Something had caused all the residents of the far northern village to leave their huts very suddenly. They never returned.

What was it? Investigations by the Northwest Mounted Police could prove nothing. Yet the police knew that no Eskimo would go anywhere distant without guns and dogs. Stranger still, a grave which once contained a body had been emptied. The stones which had covered the grave were stacked in a neat pile next to the empty hole. Animals can't stack stones.

UFO researchers believe that alien spacecraft enter the earth's atmosphere at the poles. Is it possible that there is a link between the disappearance of the inhabitants of Anjikuni and the appearance of another kind of mystery?

Lost and Found??

It was evening. The road was empty. Two young men driving to a dance saw a young girl at the side of the highway. They stopped to give her a lift. When the girl also said that she was going to a dance, the boys were delighted. They all went together.

The girl was charming. But she didn't speak much and had a mysterious manner. However, she did say that her name was Rose.

When the dance was over, the boys drove Rose home. Later, when she was gone, they realized that her scarf was still in the car.

The next day they drove back to where they had dropped off Rose to return her scarf. An old woman answered the knock. When she saw the scarf, she shuddered.

When the boys left, they drove by a graveyard nearby. There, covered with weeds, was a grave with a name on it. The name was Rose. It was as the old woman had told them. Rose, a beautiful young girl, had died many years earlier, just before a dance she swore she wouldn't miss.

A Treasure Is Waiting

When the Spanish conquistador Pizarro conquered the Incas, he captured their emperor and held him for ransom. The Incas worshiped their emperor. They agreed to pay the ransom.

Eleven thousand llamas, each carrying a load of treasure on its back, trekked across the mountains of Peru.

Before they reached the place where the ransom was to be delivered to the Spaniards, word arrived that Atahualpa, their emperor, had been slain by Pizarro.

The Incas unloaded the treasure and secretly buried it deep in the mountains. Occasionally a piece of the treasure will turn up, but the rest of the unbelievable treasure is still waiting for someone to find. Will that be all the lucky searchers find? And will they be so lucky?

The Last to Die

It was November 11, 1918. Private Henry Gunther was at the front lines with his platoon. The First World War had raged for four brutal years. Suddenly, an ambush. Private Gunther's platoon was raked by German machine-gun fire. Enraged, the young soldier charged the enemy, his bayonet flashing.

At the same instant, too far away to be heard, a messenger arrived with a startling dispatch. "The war will end at exactly 11 A.M.!" he shouted.

A shot rang out. The lethal bullet streaked across "no-man's land," the devastated area between the trenches. Private Gunther fell to the ground. The bullet had found its mark. The young infantryman was the last to die. The time was 11:01. The war was already over.

The Longest Punch

While sleeping soundly, a woman suddenly leaped from her bed holding her mouth. A powerful blow had struck her in the face.

But the room was empty. She was quite alone. Nothing stirred, not even a cat. There was no evidence that anything had fallen to punch the poor woman in the face.

What the woman didn't know was that at the very instant the blow struck her, her husband was hit in the face by the tiller of his sailboat. When he arrived home they compared their stories.

But neither to this day can explain what happened, or why.

Beware of Dreams

Robert Morris, Sr., worked for a shipping company in Maryland. One of the company's ships was due to arrive from England soon.

One night Robert Morris had a dreadful dream. He dreamed that when he went to visit the ship, he would be killed when its cannons fired a welcome salute.

When the ship did arrive, Mr. Morris refused to visit it. However, the captain convinced him that he would be safe in a small boat, out of range of the guns. The signal to fire would be a wave of the captain's arm.

Before the small boat carrying the men was out of dangerous range, the captain brushed a fly from his nose. The gunners on the ship thought it was the signal to fire.

The blast killed Robert Morris, Sr., just as he had dreamed it would.

Bail Out. . .Bail In

Flying too close to German gunfire for comfort, a World War One pilot named Makepiece put his airplane into a steep dive. The plane tilted so severely that it threw its observer out of his seat.

The unlucky observer plunged toward the ground. In the meantime, pilot Makepiece pulled out of his nosedive. There was a sudden jolt. Makepiece turned around. Hanging to the airplane's frail tail was Capt. Sedley, his observer.

Sedley climbed back into his seat where he stayed until the plane landed safely. He had fallen hundreds of feet through the sky and was surely the first airplane passenger to board his craft in mid-air.

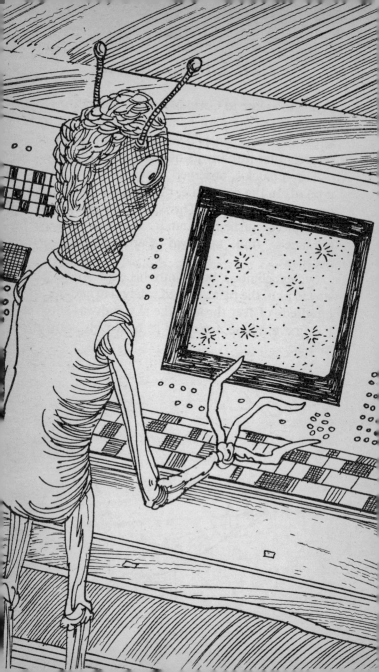

A Signal from Space?

British television watchers were astounded in September of 1953 when a television picture from the USA appeared on their screens.

In the days before satellite TV, such a feat was impossible. Yet, many people in England clearly saw the letters KLEE from Houston, Texas. Some even photographed their screens as proof.

Interested to find out why and how such a remarkable electronic miracle could be done, British television engineers wrote to station KLEE.

The reply they received stunned the engineers. KLEE had been off the air for three years. Wherever the picture had come from, it was not from Texas.

Where were the strange signals from? Is it possible that viewers not on this earth had watched them. . .and then beamed them back?

Odd Energy from the Sea

All animals produce electricity. But only a few can discharge it. The electric eel, really a fish, is one.

Eighty per cent of an electric eel's body is able to generate electric current. Produced in tiny cells, the electricity from one electric "plate," or generator, is added to the next and the next until as many as 500,000 of them are joined. This combined current is enough to knock a horse down at a distance of 20 feet. It's also enough to kill a man.

The eel uses its electricity to search for food and to stun it when it is found. It is also an excellent method of self-defense.

The Pigano

There would be no arguments from anyone if Junior refused to practice his Pigano. Here is why. Following his king's command to invent a new, unusual musical instrument, the abbot of Baigne broke all records for musical ingenuity.

Starting with a herd of pigs, from squealing little porkers to gigantic, grunting sows, the abbot rigged a keyboard attached to a series of sharp spikes. When the keyboard was played, the spikes poked the pigs. Since each key had its own spike and each spike its own pig, the result was a chorus of grunts and squeals, all under the control of the piganoist.

Even though the "pigano" was invented in the 15th Century, it's possible that the most popular piece played on it was "Pig O' My Heart."

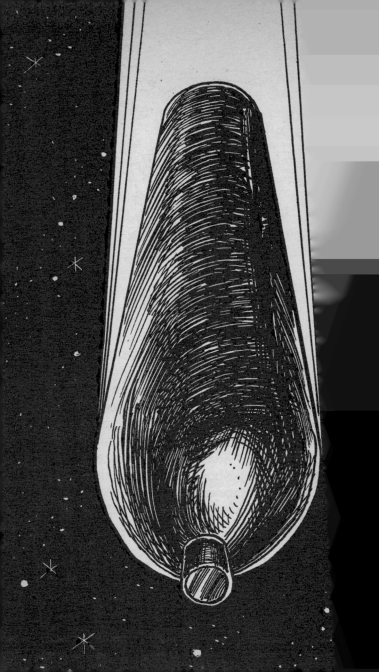

Mass Sighting???

At 11 o'clock one night Pedro Saucedo and his friend Joe Salaz were driving in Pedro's pick-up truck near Levelland, Texas. Suddenly, out of the darkness a torpedo-like machine flashed by at 800 miles per hour. The thing was ablaze.

As the strange craft buzzed the men, the truck's engine conked out. Its headlights went off. The men were left in pitch blackness. Both could feel the intense heat of the unworldly machine overhead.

When the machine blasted away into the night, the truck's lights went back on and the engine started.

Pedro called the police to report the unbelievable incident. He was worried that the police would think he was seeing things. Pedro had nothing to worry about. By morning, at least six other reports, all from different people, had been made. Each report was the same. Something from the deep, dark night sky had visited earth.

What was it? The people of Levelland could only guess.

Turtle to the Rescue

When the ship *Aloha* burned and sank 600 miles south of Manila, the Philippines, Mrs. C. Villanueva thought that she was a goner. Adrift in the ocean, far from rescue, the hapless woman floated in her life jacket, expecting the worst at any moment.

Then, to her surprise, a giant turtle emerged from the sea. It swam under her and lifted her to the surface. Another turtle, tiny by comparison, climbed to the surprised woman's back.

For two days the giant turtle carried its human passenger safely above the waves. Whenever the woman dozed off, the little turtle bit her gently to wake her up.

A rescue ship appeared. A life ring was thrown. The moment Mrs. Villanueva was safely in the life ring, the turtles swam away. But, before it made its final departure, the giant turtle circled the grateful woman twice and then vanished forever beneath the waves. Rescuers aboard the ship saw the giant turtle, but neither they nor anybody else would ever be able to explain the beast's extraordinary behavior.

O-I-L Spells Relief

Oil, not Alka-seltzer, was what one man needed to quiet a noisy stomach in 1960. It was no wonder. When doctors examined the man, who had been hospitalized, they found 258 curiosities in his stomach. Some of the noisier things included 39 nail files, 3 sets of beads, 88 coins, 26 keys and 3 pairs of tweezers.

From the "menu" removed from the man's aching stomach it could be concluded that he mistook his local hardware store for a fast food stand.

Swallowed by a Whale

The sailors in the whaleboat were terrified. Somewhere beneath them a wounded giant whale was rushing toward the surface.

The whale smashed headlong into the whaleboat, spilling the screaming men into the sea. When the water calmed down, the whale was

gone. And so were two sailors. One of them was James Bartley, a young seaman.

Many hours later the dead whale bobbed to the surface. The huge carcass was pulled alongside the ship. The work of cutting up the beast was soon underway.

When the stomach of the giant was lifted aboard the ship for processing, one of the men shouted that he had seen it move. The huge sac was carefully cut open. A man's shoe protruded from the hole, then a leg, and finally, to everyone's disbelief, a complete sailor. It was James Bartley and he was alive.

Needless to say, James Bartley didn't go to sea again, in a ship or in a whale.

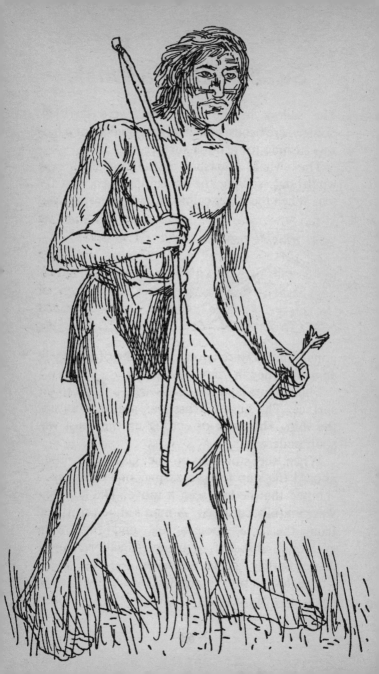

The Last Stone Age American

Unexplained stories of "wild men" living in the mountains of California were proved true when Ishi, the last American Stone Age Man, was discovered.

For years anthropologists believed that the last of the Stone Age tribes was extinct. But one, the Yana tribe, lasted into the 20th Century!

In 1911 a strange, terrified man with deer thongs in his ears and a plug of wood through his nose was captured outside the small town of Oroville, California. Named "Ishi," which means "man" in the Yana language, the primitive man was the last of his tribe.

The Yana had existed peacefully for thousands of years. But when prospectors and fortune hunters poured into Yana territory, the simple folk were hunted and killed. They were driven deep into the hills. Sadly, by 1865 there were no more than 50 left. Ishi was one of the survivors.

One by one the remainder of the tribe died. Ishi also wished to die. He was too lonely to go on.

Then he was discovered by white men. For almost 5 years he was studied by scientists. He learned many of the white man's ways. Then, in 1915, Ishi became ill with tuberculosis. When he died his primitive bow and arrows were cremated with his remains. The inscription on his burial stone says simply: *Ishi, The Last Yana Indian.*

The $90 Million Ice Cube

The parched regions of the world could be made to bloom if a French plan works.

The North Polar regions are covered with ice. Huge mountains of ice fall into the sea every year to become icebergs. The plan: Hitch an iceberg to powerful tugboats and tow it to the desert.

Could such a plan work? The company which proposes it thinks so. By tugging an 85 million ton block of ice (which is frozen *fresh* water) to any country willing to spend $90 million for the world's largest ice cube, the berg could be tapped to turn the desert green.

Signposts for
Space Travellers?

You can see them only from the air. They are gigantic lines etched across the dusty earth near Nasca, Peru. Some are merely lines. Others depict huge creatures: whales, spiders, birds. But who made them, and why, remains a complete mystery.

The Nasca lines, as the strange markings are called, were discovered only after man learned to fly above the earth in airplanes. Seen from the ground, they are simple furrows in the earth or areas cleared of stones.

Many theories have been proposed. One, the strangest of all, suggests that the huge symbols were made to guide space travellers visiting earth from other planets. If this is true could someone be using them now?

The Strange Survivor

The ship was doomed. Passengers and crew numbered over 80 people. One man looked at the boiling sea. . .and hoped he would be spared.

It was the 5th of December in 1664. It was the last day on earth for the foundering ship in the

Menai Strait. When the ship disappeared beneath the waves, one person survived. His name was Hugh Williams.

One hundred and twenty-one years later, another ship slipped beneath the waves. One man leaped into the sea to be saved. All the others perished. The man's name was Hugh Williams. The date was the 5th of December.

Seventy-five years after that, a man named Hugh Williams eyed the savage sea as his ship foundered and sank. 25 people perished. Hugh Williams survived. It was the 5th of December.

Three times on three ships in 196 years, three men named Hugh Williams survived three ship-wrecks which claimed 166 people. Each wreck occurred on the 5th of December.

Is it possible that all three men were the same?

The Strangely Empty Grave

John Gebhard was unjustly accused of robbery and murder. He was sentenced to be hanged. As a priest began to read the usual services before his execution, John Gebhard spoke up.

"I am innocent," he said. "No grave shall ever hold me. . ."

Gebhard was buried in a sealed coffin. A guard was stationed at the grave.

A short while later another man confessed to the crime. It was true. Gebhard was innocent. A decision was made to re-bury him in holy ground.

When John Gebhard's grave was opened, his body was gone. His final vow had come true.

Invasion of the Killer Bees

In 1955 a mild breed of European honeybees was crossed with an aggressive strain of bees from Africa. The result: Killer Bees.

The so-called Killer Bees first appeared in Brazil. They expanded their territory rapidly, spreading about 200 miles per year. Some people fear that they may invade the United States. But experts point out that the Killer Bees cannot adapt to temperate climates.

What makes the Killer Bees so ferocious? Scientists have concluded that they may not be any more dangerous than certain other breeds. But the fact that they swarm in giant clusters may be the reason that they are so feared. When the bees smell the scent of the chemical that they leave when they sting a victim, they swarm to it. Hundreds of bee stings can be fatal to an animal or to a person. This is reason enough to fear the "Invasion of the Killer Bees."

The Smallest Army Fights the Shortest War

When the sultan of Turkey declared war on the British Empire in 1914, two Turks living in Australia decided that it was their duty to fight for their country. An ice cream vendor and a butcher, the two men lugged guns and ammunition into the country. They decided to attack a railroad train filled with families on an outing.

Their deadly fire killed innocent passengers. Australian police and militiamen raced to the scene. The two men refused to surrender. Waving a Turkish flag they had made from a tablecloth, the two patriots held off their "enemy" until deadly gunfire cut them down. The "battle" lasted six hours. When it was over, the world's smallest army no longer existed.

Mystery Ship. . .
Mystery Crew

The *Seabird*, sails fully set, blew in from the sea toward sharp-edged rocks in full view of a helpless crowd. At the last moment a giant swell lifted the ship over the reef. It drifted to shore, unscratched.

The crowd which had gathered waited for the crew to appear. But the decks were silent. The ship was abandoned.

Boiling coffee bubbled in a pot in the galley. The captain's log had a note made only two miles away from the reef. A lone dog wandered the empty decks. Somehow, for an unknown reason, the entire crew had vanished within sight of land.

The ship's cargo was emptied. The *Seabird* lay on the beach, abandoned. Then, a few days after the mysterious grounding, it too vanished. Neither the ship nor the crew were ever seen again.

Does the *Seabird* still sail the foggy seas like the fabled *Flying Dutchman*? Like the ocean's many mysteries, the answer may lie just over the distant horizon. . .too far to be seen.

Now is the Hour

A French physician, Dr. Geley, paid a visit to one of his patients. The man was in excellent health. However, he made a strange prediction to the doctor.

"On All Saint's Day, I shall die," the man said. "Exactly at midnight." All Saint's Day was 8 days off. The man was so healthy that his claim made no sense at all.

Then, at the stroke of midnight on the fated day, the man rolled over in bed, pointed to the clock, and died.

Dr. Geley could not explain the mystery. Nor could anyone else.

Save Him from his Friends

Draco was a lawgiver in ancient Greece. He was quite strict. Some of the laws he favored were very harsh.

But many of the citizens of Athens still liked Draco. In fact, they liked him so much that they decided to honor him with a huge ceremony.

Thousands of well-wishers showed up to salute Draco at the open air arena of Athena. To show

their support and affection for their favorite lawgiver, they tossed their hats and cloaks at him, a gesture of respect in those ancient times.

Soon Draco was completely buried by heaps and heaps of heavy cloaks. Before he could be dug out, he suffocated and died.

Draco's enemies could not have done a better job getting rid of the poor man than his friends did.

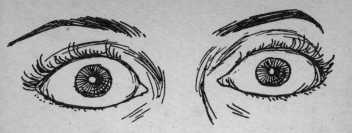

Who Was Bridey Murphy?

The hypnotist said it would be an experiment. His subject, a young woman named Virginia, was in a hypnotic trance.

"What is your name?" the hypnotist asked.

"Bridey Murphy," Virginia answered.

The woman who called herself "Bridey Murphy" described her childhood in Ireland. She used words which were common in Ireland and no place else. She told the hypnotist what her house looked like and she described her husband. She mentioned the name of her friendly, neighborhood grocer. And then she described a deadly fall down a flight of stairs. . .which led to her death.

The woman named Virginia and the hypnotist were friends in Colorado, U.S.A., in 1952. "Bridey Murphy" claimed that she was born in 1798 and that she died in 1864. Virginia had never been to Ireland, yet she had described many things there.

If Virginia was a housewife in Colorado in 1952, who was Bridey Murphy?

The Sailors Who Came Back

Tragedy struck the huge oil tanker as it neared the Panama Canal. Two men cleaning an empty cargo hatch suffocated when overcome by gases deep inside the ship. They were buried at sea.

A few days later as the sun was going down, a sailor saw something peculiar in the water on the same side of the ship from which the men had been buried. Two heads, the faces of the dead seamen in full sight, hung eerily in the waves.

Many men on the ship saw the strange faces. To end speculation about what they were, photographs were taken.

When the photos were developed, one of them showed the faces of two men. Were they the same two men who died? And if they were, why were they there? Are there ghosts in the sea? Apparently there are.

Man-sized Hailstones

In 1930, five German glider pilots were practicing in their motorless craft, because their nation was forbidden to have an air force. Suddenly, they were caught in severe weather. They were high above the mountains, yet they had no choice. They had to bail out.

The five men plummeted to earth, waiting to reach lower altitudes before opening their parachutes. But a severe updraft caught them. Like feathers, they were thrown high into the bit-

ter cold tops of giant storm clouds, the same kind that produce hail. Doused with freezing rain, the men were coated with a thin layer of ice.

Up and down the men plunged and flew. The currents in the storm tossed them like popping corn on a skillet. But with each pop they grew a thicker coat of ice.

Finally they hurtled earthward, encased in ice. Their chutes opened, but for four of the five it was too late. They were frozen to death—human hailstones.

The Man Who
Thought Pictures

Ted Serios was an ordinary enough person in 1969. However, he claimed to possess a strange and unproven ability. Serios claimed that he could project images he saw in his mind onto the film in a Polaroid held near his face.

When the method was tested, blurred, poorly focussed pictures of buildings, very real buildings, were developed on the film.

Did Ted Serios actually project images from his mind onto the film? Nobody knows. But the fact that there were pictures is a real fact. Where did they come from?

The Price of Beauty

A perfect complexion has been admired from the
earliest times. Lady Coventry was no different
from the other women of England.

To ensure a spotlessly clear complexion, Lady
Coventry regularly painted her face pure white
with a substance called white lead, an ingredient
in many paints even in modern times.

What Lady Coventry didn't know was that the
lead was deadly. The price she paid for her vanity
was high, for the lead was absorbed through her
skin and killed her.

Did Lady Coventry realize she was painting a
ghost? Her own?

200 Previews of Disaster

On October 21, 1966, a huge pile of rain-soaked tailings from local coal mines suddenly collapsed in an avalanche. The thick river of muck raced toward the town. In its path were houses, streets, and the Pantglas Junior and Infants School.

Two million tons of devastation struck the town. The school was buried. 145 people perished.

Even before it happened, 200 people already suspected the worst. They were from all over

England. The one thing they had in common was a dream. All had dreamed of the tragedy before it ever struck.

How is such a thing possible? How can 200 people see into the future? These are questions without answers.

The Abominable Snowman

The Himalayan Mountains contain some of the most inaccessible places on earth. Remote, and extremely high in altitude, very little could live there even if it chose to. But something does. And for 500 years nobody has figured out what it is. It is the yeti, the abominable snowman.

What is this strange creature?

People who claim to have seen him say he looks like certain apes. Some say he is a small, hairy beast who walks upright like a man. Others claim the yeti is huge. They say he is covered with monkey-like fur. He has a mouth filled with giant teeth. His head comes to a peculiar point. He has feet which are twelve inches long and over seven inches wide.

There is no *known* creature in the Himalayas that matches such a description. But the Sherpas, those people who live in the vast mountains, say he is real. Photographs of his giant footprints have been made. Perhaps soon the elusive, mysterious snowman will have his whole picture taken. Until then, the yeti, whatever it is, will be safe.

The Island That Comes and Goes

An explorer named Bouvet first discovered it in 1739. It was an ice-covered island near Antarctica. He named it Bouvet Island, after himself. He might have named it Vanishing Island.

When another group of explorers searched for the island many years later, it was gone. And so, the island was removed from the maps sailors use and was forgotten. But in 1808 Bouvet Island

reappeared, just where it had "always" been. It was put back on the maps. As proof that it was there, a group of British seal hunters even landed on the island.

But about 30 years later it disappeared again. Once more the elusive island was taken off the charts. Then, in 1855, three separate ships spotted the island. It went back on the charts.

The island is still there. There are even photographs of it. However, in 1921, mariners were still not so sure because the strange island once more eluded discovery.

Is Bouvet Island really there? Yes! And no.

Save the Sun

The sun is in no danger of extinction. But if it were, the earth would be in trouble in the time it takes to cook four two-minute eggs.

Light from the sun reaches the earth in eight minutes. If it were known that the sun was going to go out, and if *all* of the earth's fuel resources could be gathered and used in some kind of gigantic furnace to heat the earth, there would be only enough fuel to last for three days.

If you see a bumper sticker that says, "Save the Sun," you'll know why.

The Mummy Mystery

Two gold prospectors stared into the stone cave they had just blasted open. It was small, with just enough room to move around in. When the dust from their blasting settled down, the two men discovered that they were not alone. Sitting on a ledge was the tiny mummy of a man-like creature. The mummy sat cross-legged. It had its arms folded neatly in its lap. One eye looked as if it were winking.

Scientists studied the mummy. It was barely 14 inches tall and weighed less than a pound. X-rays disclosed a full set of bones and teeth. The investigators estimated that the tiny creature had been about 65 years old when it died.

Was it really a tiny man? Was it a relic of someone or something that lived in North America thousands of years ago? Nobody knows, and the mummy will never tell.

The Little Girl
Nobody Knows

The circus was in town. Hot July sun beat down on the Ringling Brothers, Barnum & Bailey Big Top in Hartford, Connecticut.

Suddenly, someone screamed. "Fire!"

The tent was ablaze within minutes. In a quarter of an hour it was burned to the ground. 168 people died in the tragic blaze.

Among the victims was a little girl. Her face was peaceful and unmarred. Nobody came to claim her body. A photograph was made. Newspapers across the nation carried it. And still, nobody came.

To this day nobody knows who the little girl was. *Nobody.*

Unidentified
Underwater Saucer

As the steamship *Bintang* plowed through the ocean off the coast of Sumatra, its captain saw a sight unlike any he had ever seen in years at sea.

A bright beam of light, like a searchlight's beam moved under the sea near the ship. Another similar beam approached, and then another. A huge wheel of light was slowly passing near the ship. It was very deep, but its spokes were brightly lighted.

In the center of the wheel was a lighted hub. The captain stared in disbelief as the huge wheel revolved slowly out of sight. It was never seen again. Was it a deep-sea "flying saucer"? To this day, nobody really knows.

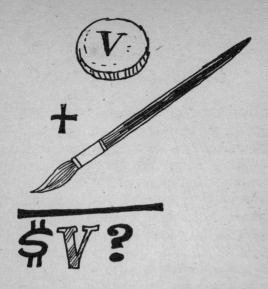

Turning Nickel into Gold

In the 1880's the U.S. nickel had the Roman numeral V on it. Naturally, V stands for 5. But the nickel didn't say 5 *what*.

Joshua Tatum noticed the interesting fact. He also came up with an ingenious plan. He took a bagful of nickels to a jeweler who plated the 5¢ pieces with a thin layer of gold. The rough edges were also removed. The result looked very much like a $5 gold piece.

Before he was caught, Tatum made a small fortune by purchasing 5¢ items in stores and then quietly accepting the $4.95 change the clerks gave him.

But, he *was* caught.

Strange Visitors from . . .?

Bill Taylor, visiting his friends, the Suttons, near Hopkinsville, Kentucky, stepped out of the house for a drink of cold water from the well. To his astonishment, a spaceship landed in a nearby field. He raced into the house.

Within minutes the house was surrounded by a strange army of 3-foot tall creatures with round heads, elephant-like ears and narrow slits for mouths. The beings had no necks and their long arms ended in clawed hands.

For hours the odd visitors roamed around the house. The people inside were terrified. Nothing they did could make the creatures leave. When one was shot with a shotgun blast, it got up and walked away.

At last the family escaped in the car. But when they returned with the deputy sheriff and two state policemen, no trace of the unbelievable visitation remained.

Who were the strange visitors? Where had they come from? And when will they return?

A Deathly Stroll

A young Australian woman was casually strolling through a neighborhood park one pleasant day when she was suddenly overcome by terror.

The woman cringed. She was overwhelmed by a feeling of terrible suffering. There was nothing physically wrong with her, but she felt mortally endangered.

To her relief, the feeling passed. But its memory was still vivid one week later when an airplane crashed at the exact spot she had stopped in the park when the strange sensation came over her. The plane's pilot suffered an agonizing death.

The woman had sensed the disaster a full week before it happened. How? That is the question.

The Man Who Flew

The old television show, *The Flying Nun,* was nothing compared to the original flying priest. Giuseppe Desa wanted to become a priest. He believed that suffering would make him worthy of his calling. He wore rough clothing which hurt his skin. He beat himself with sharp thorns.

One day while he was in a strange trance, Friar Joseph Maria, as he came to be called, suddenly became airborne. He floated in the air in full view of many witnesses.

The unusual priest lifted off on invisible wings many times. He hovered in front of crowds, he

flew before prominent people, and he soared through churches filled with worshipers. Many, many responsible people claimed that they saw the remarkable flights.

How did the peculiar priest learn to fly? Nobody knows. But one might ask, "If he really did fly, can I?"

A Real Nightmare

Newspaperman Byron Somes was sleeping in his office. He awoke with a start from a terrible dream. In the dream Byron Somes saw a huge mountain, a volcano, explode. He heard the screams of victims trapped by the awesome blast. Details of a huge disaster had come to him in his sleep. Somes wrote them all down.

Later, when he was out of his office, the first reports of an eruption somewhere halfway around the world trickled in. Someone found Somes' notes. The notes were thought to be an account of the disaster.

When it was discovered that Somes' notes were about a dream and could not possibly be true, Somes was fired for making up a preposterous story.

Then the truth became known. Krakatoa, a volcanic island, had disintegrated in the biggest explosion ever recorded to have occurred on the face of the earth. And Byron Somes had seen it all in a dream.

Can dreams come true? Byron Somes' dream was one that did.

Burpo-Fuel

A group of Texas researchers may have solved the energy crisis. Cow burps, they say, belch some 50 million tons of combustible hydrocarbons into the atmosphere each year. If the burps could be caught and stored, all of that "hot air" could be used to heat homes. The researchers calculate that burps collected from ten average cows could heat a small house for a year. The question is, who could sleep with ten cows burping in the basement?

Cancelled Voyage

J. Middleton of England was booked for a trip to New York on the world's greatest ship, the *Titanic*. The voyage would be the first ever for the magnificent vessel.

But J. Middleton had two disturbing dreams. He saw the mighty ship go down. In his dreams he seemed to be floating above the doomed ship. Rather than take a chance, Mr. Middleton cancelled his voyage.

The night before the splendid boat was scheduled to dock in New York harbor, it sliced into a giant iceberg and sank. Over 1500 passengers and crew died, while only a few over 700 survived. One who did survive was not a passenger. Mr. J. Middleton had already cancelled what would have been his final voyage.

Strange Bend in the River

The *Iron Mountain* was a huge river steamboat. It chugged up the wide river one sunny day, pulling a long string of barges behind it. The boat carried barrels of molasses, bales of cotton, and a full crew. The captain blew a long blast on the steam whistle as the lumbering giant rounded a curve in the river.

Two hours later the barges the *Iron Mountain* had been pulling drifted back down the river. The tow line connecting them to the paddle-wheeler had been cut.

The river was searched for the boat. It was gone. No wreckage was ever found. No witnesses had seen its fate. The *Iron Mountain* simply vanished, without a trace.